Thank You

We wish to thank all the instructors of Cycle Training UK fc their contribution and imagination in developing and triall these games, Ian Pearson for his guidance and Will Melling tor the beautiful photographs.

This book was compiled by instructors from Cycle Training UK. We would be grateful for any feedback about this book or ideas for new cycling games for future editions. Please email info@cycletraining.co.uk with your comments.

A special thank you to the pupils of Southfield Primary School in Ealing for agreeing to be photographed playing the games.

A huge thank you also to Cathy Gaulter-Carter, for her insightful editing and to Jonathan Spearman-Oxx for his innovative design and artwork.

Published by Cycle Training UK

David Dansky
Head of Training & Development
Cycle Training UK Ltd
The Biscuit Factory
Unit 215, Building J
100 Clements Road
London SE16 4DG
Telephone 020 7231 6005
Fax 020 7394 0624
www.cycletraining.co.uk

Competitive games

Co-operative games

Cycling games are fun! The main aim of these games is to promote cycling. Learning through games provides a fun way of practising and improving bike control skills.

Who is this book for?
This book can be used by teachers, parents, youth leaders, cycling instructors in fact by anyone who wishes to organise or play games on bicycles.

Why play cycling games?
Games may be mentally and/or physically challenging and encourage interaction between people. Some of these games are co-operative games which encourage teamwork, creative thinking and problem solving. They help players realise that everyone can win. Riding a bike on roads involves co-operating with other road users through observations, keeping to a set of agreed rules, reacting to other people's behaviour and keeping calm in all situations. Many of these skills can be practised in the playground through playing games co-operatively.

How do I teach cycling games?
Cycling games are best played on a hard surface such as a playground or tennis court (though some may be played on grass if there is no other option). You can make use of playground line markings for many of the games or you can use chalk as an alternative. Cones are useful for some of the games, otherwise you can use whatever is available – water bottles, bags or panniers.

Keep explanations short and clear. Show the riders how to play where possible. Start the game even if some players do not understand, they will learn by watching and doing. The golden rule with games is to stop playing long before the young people are bored. Change games every four or five minutes.

How do I use this book?
Each double page consists of a description the game, the rules and some hints as to managing risk while playing. Opposite the description of each game are visuals to support the explanations.

Participants   Instructors

Emergency stop race

The winner is the first person to stop over the finish line.

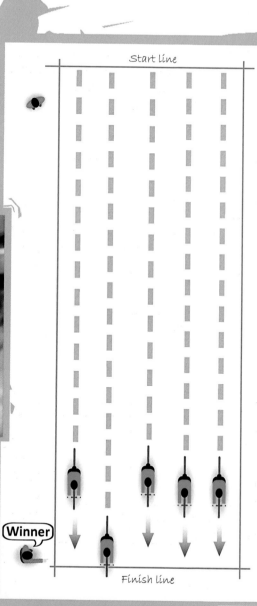

How to play Emergency stop race

What skills are practised?
- Starting
- Stopping
- Using gears

Planning
- Large enough space is required preferably with line markings for the start and finish line. The start/finish and turning line needs to be at least three metres from any wall, railing or fence.
- There must be enough room for riders to start with at least a metre between each rider.

Equipment
- Chalk if there are no line markings.

The rules
- The winner is the first person to stop with part of their bike over the finish line.
- Riders line up on the start line leaving an arm's length between each person.
- They race to the finish line stopping with part of their bike on the finish line.
- The first person to stop on the finish line wins the race.

Variations
- Riders can cycle to the end of the playground, turn round and race back to the start line.
- The first person to stop with part of their bike over the start line wins the race.

Risk management

Risk	Likelihood	Action
Riders crash into wall/fence.	Medium	• Run the game only when riders have good braking skills. •Ensure that the finish line is at least 3m from any immovable hazard such as a wall.
Riders crash into each other.	Low	• Ensure enough room between riders. • If there are too many riders, run heats.

Dodge

Trainees practise close control. The winner is the last person riding within a space that gets smaller.

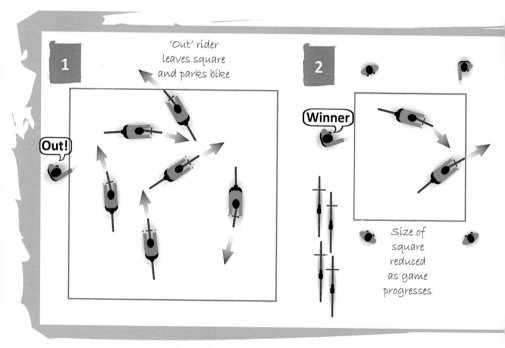

How to play Dodge

What skills are practised?
- Close control
- Braking
- Swerving
- Looking all around

Planning
- Define an area in a playground large enough for riders to cycle around freely.
- The winner is the last person riding in a space. Make the space smaller as the game progresses. Do this by moving the markers in and getting riders who are 'out' to define the space.

Equipment
Use playground markings, cones or chalk to help define the area.

The rules
- Don't cross the borders.
- Keep your feet on the pedals.
- Don't bump into or touch another rider.
- When you are out, leave the area quickly, park your bike (where instructed) then join the others to help mark the area.

Variations
- Play using differently shaped areas such as circles/ triangles
- Allow the winner to start the next game by shouting '3-2-1 Dodge!'

Risk management

What could happen	Likelihood	Action
Trainees crash.	Medium	• Run game only when riders have good control skills. • Start with a large space. Control the size of space based on number of riders still 'in'. • Ensure riders understand that they are 'out' if they bump into anyone else.
Riders who are 'out' disrupt game.	Medium	• Encourage 'out' riders to leave game area quickly. • Tell them in advance what to do with their bikes when they are out. • Ask them to join you marking the area.

Slow race

The winner is the last person to cross the finish line.

Start Line

Riders stop if they put their foot down go sideways or ride into someone

Winner!

Finish Line

Riders stop if they pass the finish line

How to play Slow race

What skills are practised?
- Close control
- Covering and pumping brakes
- Consistent pedalling cadence in low gear

Planning
- The winner is the last person to cross the finish line.
- Riders have to follow a set of rules.
- Playground with lines to indicate start and finish points.
- Play the game over a short distance.

Equipment
- None

The rules
- Keep moving forward.
- Keep your feet on the pedals.
- If you put a foot down, ride sideways/backwards, you are out and you must stop where you are. Keep brakes covered.

Variations
- For advanced riders, try a one-handed slow race.

Risk management

Risk	Likelihood	Action
Riders crash.	Medium	• Run game only when players have good skills. • Ensure large space between riders. • Ensure players understand that they are out if they bump into anyone else.
Trainees who are 'out' disrupt game.	Medium	• Encourage players who are out to remain stationary where they were called 'out'.

Grandmother's footsteps

The winner is the first person to creep up to a finish line.

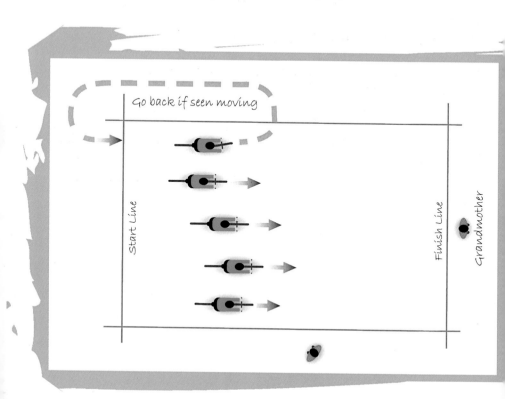

How to play Grandmother's footsteps

What skills are practised?
- Starting
- Stopping
- Close control
- Balancing

Planning
- The winner is the first person to ride slowly to the finish line without 'Grandmother' seeing him or her moving.
- Assemble riders with bikes on the start line.
- One leader watches riders and gives tips during the game.
- 'Grandmother' stands on a finish line some distance away, facing away from riders.

Equipment
- Use the lines on the playground or markers.

The rules
- The game starts when 'Grandmother' says so and turns around. You have to try to cycle up to her without Grandmother seeing you.
- If Grandmother turns round, you must stop where you are.
- If Grandmother sees you moving, you have to go back to the start line.

Risk management

Risk	Likelihood	Action
Riders crash during the game.	Low	• Space riders apart at the start line. • Monitor riders.

Out and back race

Individual members of two teams race over a course.
(This isn't a relay race!)

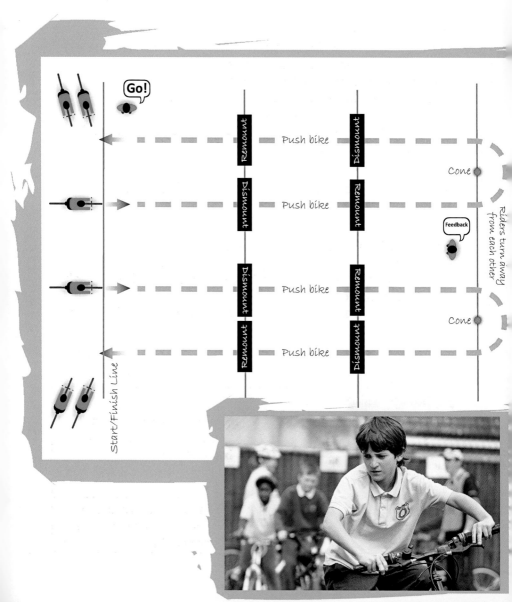

How to play Out and back race

What skills are practised?
- Setting off
- Pushing the bike
- Mounting and dismounting
- Accurate stopping
- Using gears

Planning
- Prepare two parallel 'out and back' courses, one for each team.
- You need a start/finish line with overrun space behind it.
- After several metres there should be a dismount line.
- After several more metres there should be a remount line.
- Then there should be turnaround point.
- Divide the group in to two teams. Choose teams so that more skilled riders are divided between both teams.

Equipment
- Markers or cones for the turnaround points. Chalk if there are no playground markings.

The rules
- Two people, one from each team, race each other.
- The first back over the line scores one point for their team.
- The team members who are waiting their turn need to stand back to make space for the finishing riders.
- Between the dismount and remount sections riders must push their bike.

Variations
- If there is lots of space, additional obstacles can be added to the course.

Risk management

Risk	Likelihood	Action
Riders crash into fellow team members at finish line.	Low	• Riders briefed to keep area clear. Instructor monitors and manages riders who are waiting. NB Do not attempt to organise this as a relay race.
Rider trips or falls when pushing the bike.	Low	• Keep the 'on foot' section short so that riders cannot build up to much speed running with the bike.

Obstacle race

Riders from two teams complete a short obstacle course.

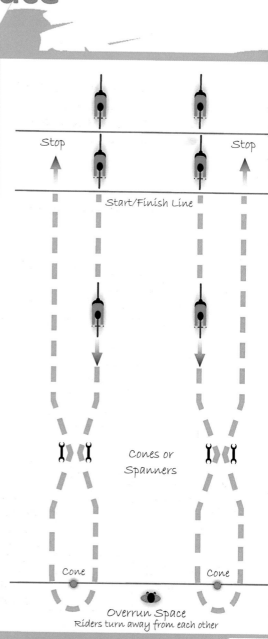

Stop

Stop

Start/Finish Line

Cones or Spanners

Cone

Cone

Overrun Space
Riders turn away from each other

How to play Obstacle race

What skills are practised?
- Close control
- Balance
- Using gears

Planning
- Set up two cones or spanners 10m-15m from a starting line in a playground. Place about 20cm apart then place an object such as a water bottle for riders to go round four paces beyond the cones.
- Repeat this arrangement in parallel along the playground for the second team.

Equipment
- Chalk if there are no playground markings.
- Cones or spanners and two water bottles.

The rules
- Divide riders into two teams.
- One rider from each team cycles between the cones, around the water bottle then back between the cones to return to the starting line.
- The first one to stop on the finish line earns a point for their team. If you hit an obstacle or overshoot the finish line, you don't get the point.

Variations
- Vary the distance between the obstacles and length of the course.
- Be strict about how to end the race and award additional points if riders stop with the front wheel on the finish line.
- Vary the points system i.e. award two points for the first back and deduct one point for hitting an obstacle.

Risk management

Risk	Likelihood	Action
Riders crash while going round the obstacles.	Low	• Ensure that the obstacles are well spaced out initially, perhaps making the course more challenging as riders' skills improve.
Riders crash racing to the finish line.	Low	• Riders must stop with part of their bike on the finish line in order to get the point.

Four squares

The winner is the rider remaining after successive rounds of elimination by a blindfolded 'Judge'.

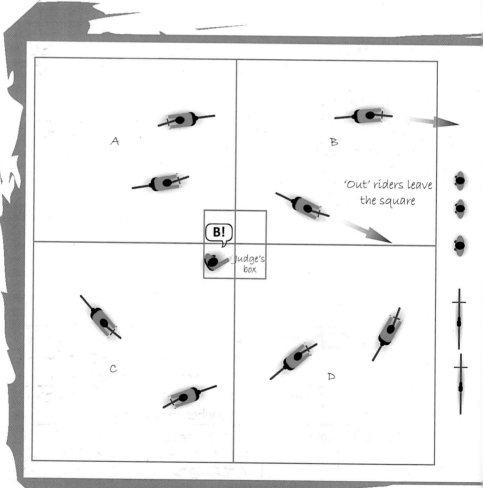

How to play Four squares

What skills are practised?
- Close control
- Smooth braking
- Manoeuvring

Planning
- Define an area large enough for players to ride around freely and divide it into four equal-sized squares or rectangles.
- Draw a square in the centre about 1m square. This is the Judge's box.

Equipment
- Blindfold and chalk for markings on playground

The rules
- There are four areas, A, B, C and D.
- In the centre of these four areas will be the Judge who will be blindfolded.
- You will be riding around these four areas until the Judge begins counting down from five to zero.
- When the count finishes, you must stop in a square.
- The Judge will then call out A, B, C or D. All those in that square are out. We keep playing until there is only one person remaining or everyone is out.
- Riders will also be 'out' and must leave the area if...
  1. You bump into or touch another rider.
  2. You ride outside the four squares.
  3. You ride inside the Judge's box.
- When you are out, leave the area quickly, park your bike and watch the game.

Variations
- Allow the winner to become the Judge.
- Set number of rounds and to allow for several winners.

Risk management

Risk	Likelihood	Action
Riders crash.	Medium	• Ensure riders understand that they are 'out' if they bump into anyone else.
Riders who are 'out' disrupt game.	Medium	• Tell them in advance what to do with bikes when they are out.
Riders collide with the Judge.	Low	• Have a space around the Judge in which riders are not allowed (the Judge's box).

Follow the leader

Riders cycle in a line behind a leader and copy his/her actions

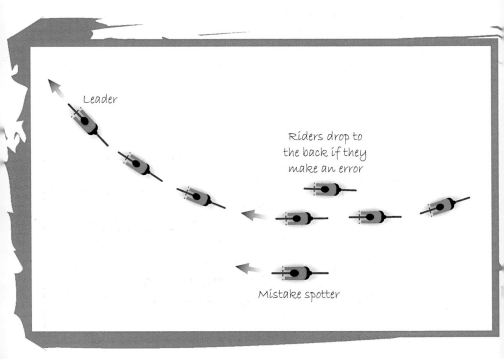

Leader

Riders drop to
the back if they
make an error

Mistake spotter

How to play Follow the leader

What skills are practised?
- Close control
- Riding in a line
- Taking a hand off the handlebars
- Preparation for group riding

Planning
- Riders learn how to ride in a line, understand the importance of keeping enough room between them and the person in front.

Equipment
- None

The Rules
- Riders cycle in a line behind the leader.
- They copy what the leader does.
- The leader will perform various actions i.e. look over shoulder, put hand on head, signal or stop.
- Another person will watch for riders not copying the leader.
- In addition the 'mistake spotter' should look for...
  1. Rider not covering brakes.
  2. Front wheel overlapping with the person in front.
  3. Letting the gap get too long between riders.
  4. Not setting the pedal when setting off
- Anyone who doesn't copy the leader or makes a mistake must drop to the back of the line by moving to the right.

Variations
- Let a young person be the front rider or the 'mistake spotter'.

Risk management

Risk	Likelihood	Action
Riders crash.	Low	• Run game only when riders have good skills. • Start by moving slowly and making simple actions as riders get used to moving in a line.
The same riders make mistakes and get disheartened and lose interest.	Medium	• The 'spotter' person can manipulate who gets called out making a mistake.

Mirror image

Riders mimic the instructor's actions.

Riders wait their turn

Start line

Start line

Riders wait their turn

How to play Mirror image

What skills are practised?
• Signalling

Planning
• Make sure that there is a fairly long run up towards the person the rider is mimicking and space for the rider to cycle back to the others.

Equipment
None

The rules
• The leader stands in front of the riders.
• Riders cycle towards the leader one at a time.
• Riders watch the leader and copy you with a mirror image. So if the leader puts his/her right hand out, riders should put their left hand out.

Variations
• Make the actions easier and harder according the ability of individual riders. Someone who is not confident can lift their hand up slightly from the handlebar. Keep them looking at you all the time and count how long they have their hand off the bars.
• You can ask a rider who is very confident to pat their head.
• Make sure that each rider can do a proper signal by the end.

Risk management

Risk	Likelihood	Action
Rider falls off.	Low	• Match your action with the player's ability and build up confidence appropriately. • Keep the riders looking at you and pedalling.
Rider crashes into you.	Low	• Make sure that you put your hand back into the handlebar position before the rider reaches you / the place where they need to turn. • Make sure that there is a long enough area for this game. If necessary use the diagonal of the playground.

Swervin' Mervin

Riders make tight turns between two lines.

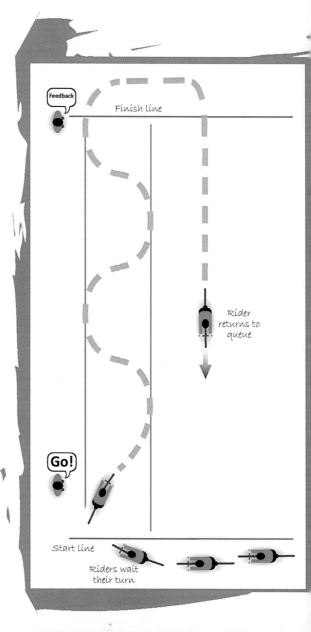

Feedback

Finish line

Rider returns to queue

Go!

Start line

Riders wait their turn

How to play Swervin' Mervin

What skills are practised?
- Tight turns
- Swerving

Planning
- Select two parallel lines (1 to 3 metres apart) running the length of the playground. One person sets off the riders, another counts the points/gives feedback at far end of the lines.

Equipment
- None

The rules
- Set off one-by-one from the end of the lines.
- Swerve from side to side so that the front tyre touches or crosses one line, then the other.
- Score one point for each complete side-to-side swerve (each time the wheel touches one of the side lines).
- At the end, come back and join the end of the queue.

Variations
- Can be used with an individual rider.

Risk management

Risk	Likelihood	Action
Rider crashes during the game.	Low	• Monitor and ensure players control their speed.
Riders riding back to the start point may crash.	Medium	• Monitor riders giving clear instructions as to the route back to the start point. • Add another task for riders which will require close control on the return leg, e.g. riding between two obstacles.

Follow the hand

Riders follow instructions by watching rather than listening.

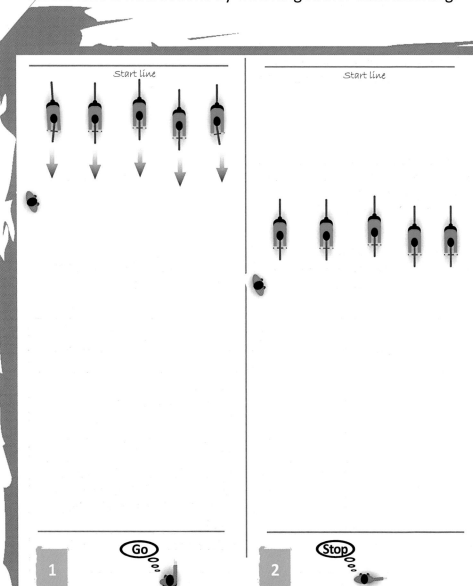

How to play Follow the hand

What skills are practised?
• Stopping with control
• Starting with pedal set
• Obeying hand signals

Planning
• Make sure that the space is large enough for the numbers of riders.
• Line up riders with plenty of space between them.
• Demonstrate 'stop' signal and 'go' signal.

Equipment
• None

The rules
• You need to obey hand signals only.
• To make it more difficult, I might say 'Stop!' but use the 'Go' signal. That means you must go.
• That means you must go!

Variations
• Wait until everyone has set their pedal before starting.
• Make it more and more difficult as they get better by mixing up hand and word commands and making them move faster and faster.

Risk management

Risk	Likelihood	Action
Riders cycle too fast.	Medium	• Keep your voice low and the verbal commands quite soft so riders have to pay attention. • Don't set them off too quickly. Don't let them ride for a long distance to avoid anyone picking up too much speed.
Riders crash into one another.	Low	• Space the riders out at the start and instruct them to ride in a straight line. If they get too close to each other, stop and start again.
Riders crash into you.		• Stop them before they get too close!

Dozy pedestrian

Riders control their bikes aiming to avoid colliding with pedestrians as they move in their path.

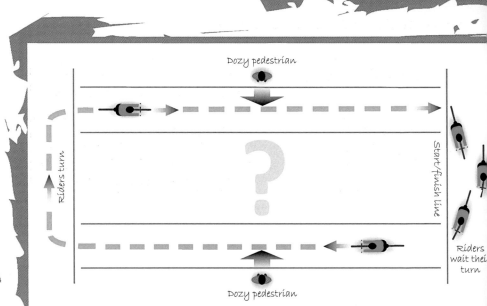

Dozy pedestrian

Riders turn

Start/finish line

Riders wait their turn

?

Dozy pedestrian

How to play Dozy pedestrian

What skills are practised?
- Emergency stop
- Swerving
- Anticipating potential hazards
- Choosing appropriate speed

Planning
- Select two parallel lines about two or three meters apart running the length of the playground.

Equipment
- None

The rules
- One-by-one, you will to be riding from here to the far end, staying between these two lines.
- We will be 'dozy pedestrians' who don't look where we are going.
- You need to be ready, and look out in case we do something stupid like step out in front of you without looking. You might have to stop, or slow down, or swerve, but you must stay between the two lines.
- Once you get to the end, ride back that way to the end of the queue.

Variations
- Escalate level of 'doziness' as riders reactions improve.

Risk management

Risk	Likelihood	Action
Rider crashes into pedestrian.	Low	• Choose the level of challenge to suit each rider's ability.
Riders cycling back to the start point may crash.	Medium	• Monitor riders. • Add another task for riders which will require close control on the return leg, e.g. riding between two obstacles.

Please let me in

Riders have to gain permission to cross into another cyclist's lane.

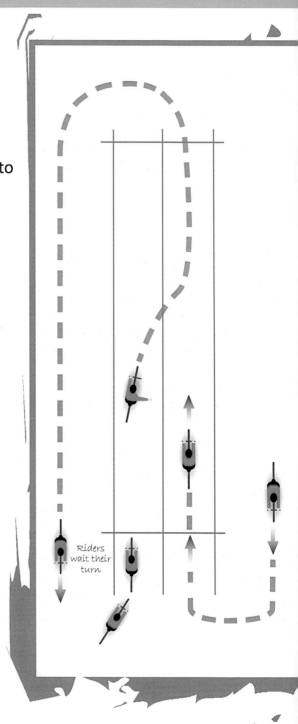

Riders wait their turn

How to play Please let me in

What skills are practised?
- Looking back
- Signalling
- Making eye contact

Planning
- Define two lanes in the playground, the longer the better.
- Leave enough room to turn at the end.

Equipment
- Use lines on playground or chalk.

The rules
- Rider sets off riding down the left hand lane.
- The leader sets off riding down the right hand lane slightly behind the rider.
- The rider looks back, makes eye contact then signals to move into the right lane in front of the leader.
- The rider can only move when the leader allows them to with a nod.
- If there is no nod, the rider cannot move right and stays in the left lane.
- At the end of the lane, the rider turns left back to the starting line.

Variations
- The leader makes it harder by not looking at the rider.
- The rider and leader can swap roles.

Risk management

Risk	Likelihood	Action
Rider wobbles and falls.	Low	• Run game when riders can look back and signal confidently. • If rider is wobbly, get them to practise more looking back and signalling before playing again.
Riders waiting their go get bored.	Medium	• Alternate with another leader so the pace of the game is faster. • Leader calls the next rider to start while riding back to the start.

Stay in the box

New rider has to ride
within a restricted area.

How to play Stay in the box

What skills are practised?

- Steering
- Riding slowly

Planning

- Define an area in a playground large enough for the rider to be able to cycle around in at low speed.

Equipment

- Use playground markings or chalk to help define area.

The rules

- Rider only allowed to cycle inside a defined area and must not cross the lines.
- If the rider puts his/her foot down he/she has to start again.

Variations

- Make the area smaller as the rider gets better.

Risk management

Risk	Likelihood	Action
Rider falls off.	Low	• Run game only when the rider is able to ride around a larger area. • Make sure that the area is small enough to keep the speed low.